WAYS TO SAY
THE WORDS
YOU'VE HEARD

by Jennifer L. Rogala

Illustrated by Pradeep

---

to Jillian and Samantha

"Ways to Say the Words You've Heard," by Jennifer L. Rogala. Illustrated by Pradeep. ISBN 1-58939-864-5.

Published 2006 by Virtualbookworm.com Publishing Inc., P.O. Box 9949, College Station, TX 77842, US. ©2006, Jennifer L. Rogala. All rights reserved. No part of this publication may be reproduced, stored in a retrieval system, or transmitted in any form or by any means, electronic, mechanical, recording or otherwise, without the prior written permission of Jennifer L. Rogala.

Manufactured in the United States of America.

How do you say hi?

Greetings, what's up, good day, hey, or wave to friends nearby.

Hawaiians say, "Aloha" on Oahu and Kauai.

How do you say teeth?

Choppers, fangs, and pearly whites, you brush them twice a day.

They say, "denti" in Venice, and "daant" in Bombay.

How do you say head?

Noggin, noodle, thinker, squash, crown, or skull, or brain,

The word for head is la cabeza in Barcelona Spain.

How do you say trousers?

Knickers, britches, blue jeans, slacks, overalls, and pants,

It's pantelone in Greece, and les pantalon in France.

How do you say shoes?

Footwear, loafers, wingtips, clogs, boots, high heels, and flip-flops,

Slippers, sandals, sneakers, cleats, moccasins, and high-tops

How do you say eat?

Gobble, nibble, pig out, chew, dine, or have a bite.

Breakfast in the morning, and dinnertime at night.

How do you say horse?

Bronco, filly, mustang, colt are all good words indeed.

Clydesdale, stallion, pony, mare, gelding, foal, and steed

How do you say yes?

Okay, of course, all right, yep, surely or instead,

You speak no words at all and just simply nod your head.

How do you say walk?

Hoof-it, toddle, march, and stride, go on foot, or pace,

Meander, roam, tread, and stroll, step, parade, and race

How do you say talk?

Chitchat, babble, tell, and gab, whisper, squawk, or squeak,

Chatter, utter, say, and tell, verbalize, or speak

How do you say street?

Avenue, footpath, lane, and trail, road, and route, and byway,

Boulevard, alley, pavement, terrace, dead end, drag, and highway

How do you say car?

Jalopy, auto, taxi, coupe, wheels, and limousine,

Wagon, hatchback, roadster, van, jeep, and driving machine

How do you say song?

Ballad, ditty, rock and roll, rhythm, tune, and music,

Golden oldie, chorus, anthem, melody, and lyric

How do you say bug?

Insect, spider, cootie, ant, butterfly, and bee,

Mosquito, beetle, inchworm, slug, dragonfly, and flea

How do you say bird?

Tweeter, fowl, feathered friend, parrot, blue jay, hen,

Owl, falcon, eagle, stork, pigeon, dove, and wren

How do you say dog?

Canine, puppy, pooch, and hound, man's best friend, and bow-wow,

Poodle, Shepard, Husky, Pug, Terrier, and Chow-chow

How do you say fun?

Good time, playing, have a blast, pastime, romping, Wheeeeee!

Clowning, frolic, horseplay, sport, enjoyment, cheer, Whoopee!

How do you say boo-boo?

Cuts and scrapes, a bruise or bump that turns all black and blue.

In Japan when kids fall and get hurt they call it a kizu.

How do you say no?

Forget it, uh-uh, shake your head, negative, nope, and nay,

I don't think so, not right now, turn thumbs down, no way

How do you say home?

Apartment, cabin, cottage, house, villa, pad, and condo,

Dwelling, castle, ranch, and farm, nest, address, and bungalow

How do you say family?

Relatives, kin, clan, folks, your father, and your mother,

Auntie, Uncle, Grandpa, Nana, sister, and your brother

How do you say goody?

Candy, cookie, popcorn, chips, ice cream sundae, treat,

Chocolate, bonbon, cake, dessert, apple pie, and sweet

How do you say bedtime?

Slumber, shuteye, forty winks, rest, and counting sheep,

Napping, dreaming, hit the sack, snoozing, doze, and sleep

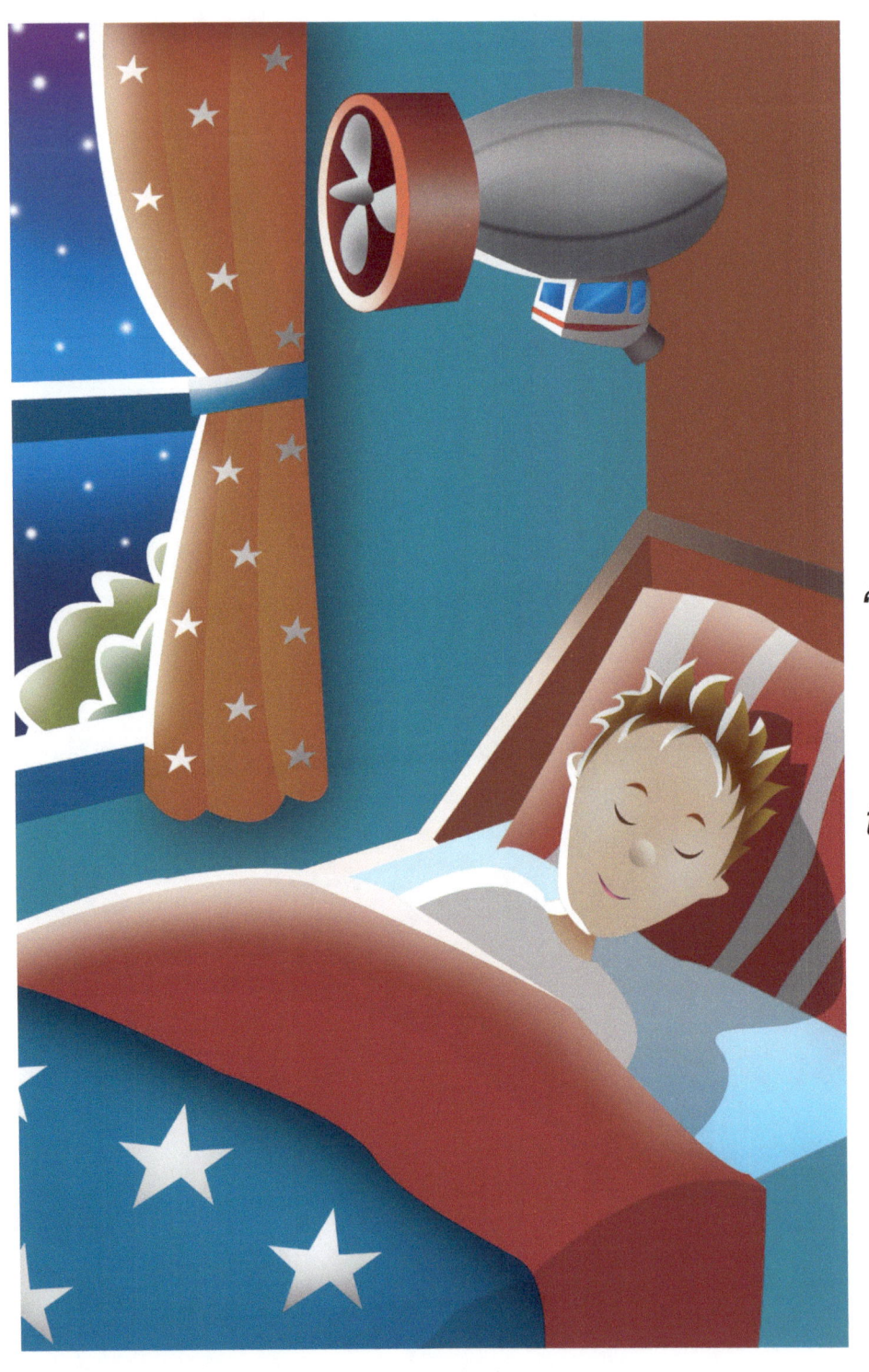

How do you say good-bye?

Hawaiians say, "Aloha" to say both bye and hi.

Farewell, so long, toodle-oo, cheerio, bye-bye.

www.ingramcontent.com/pod-product-compliance
Lightning Source LLC
Chambersburg PA
CBHW042128040426
42450CB00002B/119